Published by Creative Education
P.O. Box 227, Mankato, Minnesota 56002
Creative Education is an imprint of
The Creative Company
www.thecreativecompany.us

Design by The Design Lab
Production by Chelsey Luther
Art direction by Rita Marshall
Printed in the United States of America

Photographs by Alamy (Corbis Flirt, Greg Duncan/
Kenebec Images), Dreamstime (Isselee), Getty Images
(Oxford Scientific, Kevin Schafer), iStockphoto (jim
kruger), Shutterstock (Volodymyr Burdiak, Tony
Campbell, Eric Isselee), SuperStock (age fotostock,
Corbis, Dennis Fast VWPics, NHPA)

Library of Congress Cataloging-in-Publication Data
Riggs, Kate.
Cougars / Kate Riggs.
p. cm. — (Amazing animals)
Summary: A basic exploration of the appearance,
behavior, and habitat of cougars, the second-largest
cats of the Americas. Also included is a story from folk-
lore explaining why cougars have long, thin bodies.
Includes bibliographical references and index.
ISBN 978-1-60818-347-0
1. Puma—Juvenile literature. I. Title. II. Series:
Amazing animals.

QL737. C23R5383 2014
599.75'24—dc23   2013002870

First Edition
9 8 7 6 5 4 3 2 1

AMAZING ANIMALS
COUGARS

BY KATE RIGGS

CREATIVE EDUCATION

A cougar is a wild cat. Cougars live in North America and South America. They are smaller than other wild cats called jaguars. Some people call cougars "mountain lions" or "panthers."

Cougars are known as "catamounts" or "pumas," too

Cougars are quick cats. They have long legs and big feet. Most cougars have light brown fur. They do not have spots like some other big cats. Cougars do not roar, either. They make growling, screeching, and screaming sounds.

The cougar is good at leaping and running for short distances

Male cougars in North America weigh about 200 pounds (91 kg). Female cougars are smaller. Cougars can be taller than two feet (61 cm). Their bodies are three to six feet (0.9–1.8 m) long.

A cougar's tail is 25 to 37 inches (63.5– 94 cm) long

*A cougar can blend
in with the color of
tall grass*

Cougars can live in many different places. They can live in **swamps** and grasslands. They can live high in the **mountains** or in dark forests. They can live in dry lands called deserts and cold, snowy places, too.

mountains very big hills made of rock

swamps wet, muddy areas with a lot of plants

*Cougars hunt bigger
animals in the north and
smaller ones in the south*

Cougars eat meat. They use their teeth to grip **prey** and chew up meat. A cougar's rough tongue can lick bones clean. Cougars hunt for prey such as deer.

prey animals that are killed and eaten by other animals

It takes two and a half years for a cub to lose its spots

A mother cougar has as many as six **cubs** at a time. Cougar cubs are small at first. They have spots on their fur and rings on their tail. They drink their mother's milk. Then the mother cougar teaches the cubs how to hunt.

cubs baby cougars

Cougars stay inside their territories to look for food

Cougars in the wild live for about 15 years. They live alone in their own **territories**. These territories are called home ranges. Cougars in zoos can live for more than 25 years.

territories spaces that are the home of one animal

Cougars sleep during the daytime. They like to hunt early in the morning or at night. They follow their prey and walk around their home ranges.

Cougars curl up to rest in a safe place

Some cougars live near people in the western United States and Florida. People can see cougars in zoos, too. It is fun to see these sneaky cats up-close!

Cougars have 28 teeth, with 4 big ones called canines

A Cougar Story

Why are cougars long and thin? People in the northwestern part of America tell a story about this. The cougar used to be short and round. It was lazy and stole food. One day, the cougar stole food from Old Man, the maker of all the animals. Old Man was not happy! He pulled the cougar's tail and swung the cat around and around. Cougars have had long tails and thin bodies ever since.

Read More

Owings, Lisa. *Mountain Lion Attack!* Minneapolis: Bellwether Media, 2013.

Walker, Sarah. *Big Cats.* New York: DK Publishing, 2002.

Websites

Cougar Fund: Cougar Videos & Slideshows
http://www.cougarfund.org/channel/video/
Visit this site to see videos and pictures of wild cougars.

Enchanted Learning: Cougar
http://www.enchantedlearning.com/subjects/mammals/cats/cougar/Cougarprintout.shtml
This site has facts about the cougar and a picture to print and color.

Index